REIKI HEALING

A BOOK ON ENERGY HEALING TO HARNESS HEALTH, WEALTH AND BLISS IN LIFE

ARPANA KUMAR

Made with ♥ on the Notion Press Platform
www.notionpress.com

REIKI- 1

A STEP TOWARDS LIGHT

(DEDICATED TO MY FAMILY)

By- Arpana Kumar

Reiki Master

Contents

Foreword

The book is based on the Usui System of Healing. It is dedicated to those seekers who are ready to acquire more light, in their lives. The Reiki healing method is an ancient healing technique of Rig Veda period. It allows adept to harness more light or Prana or life force energy in their lives.

The observance of hand healing method had been practiced during Rig Veda period, by Christ and by Gautam Buddha. Thus as a science of humanity the healing method helps all who seek it willingly.

As the universe, earth, air, soil and water have no religion, in the same way the Life Force Energy and Reiki healing method are not bound by any religion. Peace and bliss is the basic right of every living being and Reiki healing method is a step towards it.

Reiki healing opens channels of joy, love and gratitude in life. These are the blissful emotions of higher consciousness. They are the fertile ground of prosperity and holistic life.

Having more light or Prana energy in life, calls for active participation by the seeker. Once equipped with self empowerment of Reiki initiation, the adept can open infinite growth in his life and make the world the best place to live in.

I hope that the book will fulfill the benevolent aspiration of mine to serve the maximum.

May this book provide insight to all who practice Reiki!

May it encourage all to acquire Reiki and have more light in their lives so that they can help and support the cause of humanity and the earth!

May everyone respond to loving teaching of Reiki and seek it!

May everyone live with the wisdom of Reiki and acquire more peace and harmony in their lives!

May the world be filled with joy, love, and gratitude! May all being be blessed!

Preface

The book is an outcome of my engagement with Reiki healing method. To enhance and aid the effect of Reiki healing, my journey of learning had started.

To understand the cause and cure of illness and life incidents, I explored science of Buddhist healing methods, Yoga, Ayurveda and Astronomy according to my capacity. I am still on the path of learning in the view of vastness of the subjects knowledge.

With my studies, Reiki healing method has been my perennial companion. At Reiki healing sessions, I have regularly been getting insights and concepts for the book.

During one of my Reiki and meditation sessions, the concept of the book came to me as, "How can I serve the best?" Based on the concept of Buddhist thought, "Dhamma" or Vedic "Dharma" which guide us that everyone of us who are on this earth has certain purpose to serve and observance of that purpose is our dharma.

According to my understanding in my own little way I am trying to serve that purpose which I received from the world. I presented my concept about energy healing method in the book. Even in future, whatever I will learn, I will share with all of you with revised editions or new books.

Acknowledgements

I wish to express my gratitude to the universe, to society and my family for making it possible for me to author this book. The world around me has been a driving force for my becoming a Reiki Master and for subsequently encouraging me to write a book on Reiki. The inputs I received from my surroundings as love, achievement, as well as concerns and apprehensions guided me to choose the path of Reiki. While walking on the path of Reiki, the joyous inquisitiveness that rose within me prompted me to further learn and explore different healing methods.

In this way, my journey of learning begun once again. My expedition as a knowledge seeker led me to various wisdoms of the world. Nevertheless, in my limited studies, Buddhist and Vedic knowledge have been instrumental to shaping my thoughts. Based on these sources of ancient wisdom, I learnt to find answers too much of my inner crisis.

Here, I would love to present before you whatever I have learnt.

For her support in writing this book, I am grateful and indebted to my daughter, a beautiful mind — the mentor of my literary journey, who stood beside me with meaningful insights and unwavering guidance. I also convey my heartfelt gratitude to my family members for their unconditional support and for being always supportive of my endeavors.

I also extend special thanks to Smt Renu Prasad for her loving and unconditional guidance in helping me launch the book and to Sri Preet Ranjan Prasad for his encouraging words and for helping me retain a positive attitude towards my work.

Prologue

The concept of the book is based upon my premonition. It would strike me whenever I had to handle urgent circumstances in my life.

My search to Reiki started when I would tend my near ones in pain. The recurrence of ailments at home prompted me to seek an aid which could take care of them. I wanted to discard the blanket of haplessness at any cost. I was ready to take responsibility to solve the problem and work for it. My search finally guided me to Reiki. Fortunately it took care of the needs of my life. At the same time, it enriched my outlook about the preciousness of life and to work on it.

How did Reiki come to me? To find something with power to cure was just a fleeting muse of my apprehensive moments. It would cross my mind, the moment I would encounter pain around me. The persistent muse of my mind was "**to search the special thing with power to cure**".

Inexplicably I was unable to give up the muse.

Eventually, it persisted and shaped as believe. But my revelation reciprocated every time with astonished expression by family members. Everyone was finding it difficult to accept my idea of **"something special with power to cure."** Lovingly, I would be suggested by them "be practical and look for practical measures."

But my consciousness was not ready to give up. The muse kept crossing with same fervor every time whenever I would see pain around me. Then I came across an article in Femina magazine. It was about a healing method of Rig Veda period. It was a hand's healing method that was practiced by Gautam Buddha. The hand healing method was briefly scripted in that article.

The brief information made me bolder. After that I escalated my search. I started asking the friends and acquaintances for teacher who knew about that way of healing. And in a fortnight, from one of my friends, I got the address of a Reiki master.

Unfortunately, due to my other commitments, I could not make it. However, one of my family members got initiated to Reiki Healing Method. And he started self healing. Although during healing he would often get sunk in great pain without any clue how to handle it. Perplexed with trouble, I realized, I need more information to handle it.

After eight months I got myself initiated in Reiki healing method. I made resolve not only to learn the method but to execute it successfully. And thus my research on Reiki and allied healing methods to Ayurveda, Yoga and Astrology and about the Lords of Hindu Pantheons went on. I am still on the path of learning. Nevertheless, till date what I learnt and understood as my earnest endeavor I would like to present before you in the form of this book.

Index

CHAPTER ONE

INTRODUCTION OF REIKI

What is Reiki ?

Reiki (Rei-universal life force; ki- energy) is a Buddhist healing method. Reiki technique enables a person to harness more life force energy in the body, mind and soul.

Aim of Reiki- Reiki heals the body, mind and soul. The strengthened self gives clarity, awareness to cause and solution to the crisis. Thus it acts as a holistic treatment in life.

Reiki initiation enables the life force energy to go deep into conscious and subconscious. Aided with five percepts of Reiki and meditation, its holistic healing equally takes care of the body, mind and soul. Thus, it incorporates easily into our behavior, as our subconscious brain is receptive to the conscious brain.

First Degree Reiki- The first degree Reiki works on the physical level. The healing subsequently shows on our relationships with the outer physical world, for instance people, thing, environment, animal and our bodies.

First Degree Reiki Initiation increases receptiveness to the universal energy. It heals the body as well as the mind.

How does First Degree Reiki function ? Or What does First Degree Reiki Initiation do ?

The First Degree Reiki attunes and aligns the life force energy of subject or adept. Initiation allows the adept to be attuned with life force energy.

Reiki healing helps to channelize the flow of universal life energy. Subsequently it harmonizes the body and mind that manifests as good health.

After initiation, the adept acquires ability to call the life force energy on his will to heal self and others. Initiation helps him to channelize life force energy in a focused way for healing.

What does First Degree Reiki Initiation do to the adept?

In First Degree initiation, four upper chakras- crown, third eye, throat and heart are initiated.

After initiation, to start healing, "Gratitude to Attitude" is offered and energy is called through the crown chakra, then to third eye chakra, to throat chakras and finally to heart chakra, next as a golden or white light ball it is brought in both the palms. At that moment the adept becomes ready to heal self and others.

It is a traditional way of initiation to attune the adept at first level to enable him to acquire healing power.

Body treatment -Self /others is a stepwise process. It is completed in following ways-

-Attitude of gratitude

-Aura cleaning

-Specific hand position to heal whole body.

-Front body healing

-Spiraling

-Back body healing

-Energy balancing

-Reiki finish

-Chakra balancing

The different points correspond to all vital organs of the body, thus the process heals the entire body. The healing corresponds to physical, mental and spiritual body.

FRONT BODY HEALING

-Heal the front body, all points while placing the hands on them.

-HEAD- Points: Right and Left Hemisphere (Right and Left sides of brain, keeping in mind that palms not to be put over Sahasrar chakra or Crown chakra). Then Eyes, ears, back of head.

-Third Eye chakra

-Throat chakra

-Heart chakra

-Solar Plexus

-Hara chakra

-Root chakra

-Knees

-Ankles

Note –To heal, curve the palm in bowl shape (fingers joined).

SPIRALING

On completion of frontal body, draw anti-clockwise energy spirals (write or draw with two fingers- index finger and middle finger numeral 6). It should be started from shoulders down the arms to the fingertips and from shoulders down along the side of the body to the tips of the toes.

BACK BODY HEALING-

Healing of all chakras:

-Back of head (upper, middle and lower brain, brain stem)

-Throat chakra

-Heart chakra

-Solar Plexus

-Hara chakra

-Root chakra

-knee

-Ankle

ENERGY BALANCING (OTHERS)

1. Have the client lie on his stomach.
2. Put one hand on the neck (one inch above the body) and feel its energy.
3. Put the other hands on the root chakra (one inch above the body) and feel its energy.

4. Bring both the hands in the center and balance the energy.
5. SWEEPING

    a. Form V with two fingers and place them at the base of the neck and pull down along the spine to the base of the spine (if the client is non-diabetic).

    b. If the patient is diabetic, the stroke should be from the base of the spine to base of the neck.

The Reiki treatment is now complete.

CHAKRA BALANCING (SELF)

For twenty-one days, give full body treatment (at all points for three minutes). It can be completed in two or three sittings.

If one cannot do full body treatment due to some unavoidable reasons, do chakra balancing as follows:

a. Put right palm on the back of the fore head and the left palm on the Root Chakra.
b. After three minutes, move the right palm to the third eye chakra, move left palm to Hara chakra from Root Chakra.
c. After three minutes, move the right palm to throat chakra and left palm to Solar Plexus Chakra.
d. After three minutes, move the right palm to Heart Chakra and left palm also to Heart Chakra.
e. So within fifteen minutes, the Chakras are balanced.

SHORT TREATMENT (SELF AND OTHERS)

It can be done on chakras level by placing left hand on back and right hand on front for the healing.

- Third Eye Chakra
- Throat Chakra
- Heart Chakra
- Solar Plexus Chakra
- Hara Chakra

- ∘ Root Chakra
- ∘ if time permits - knee Chakra and ankle Chakra.

To heal others-family, friends, plants, animals, food and water can also be healed.

REIKI FINISH

When the Reiki session is complete, the healer should wash his palm and fingers or press his finger tips together for 30 seconds to close down the energy flow.

Discussions on Reiki

Benefit and need of group Reiki healing- Usually group healing is recommended to a person having acute/serious ailments that could otherwise take a long time to cure. Group healing enables the person to recover fast.

Aids of Reiki -These practices facilitate Reiki healing:

-Meditation Prayer

-Positive Thoughts Affirmations

-Guided visualization and breathing.

Reiki affirmation- How to do it?

-Close the eyes.

-Cease the thoughts.

-Come in witness and detached mode.

-Don't react or yield to recall of any unfavorable incidents and thoughts, just be a witness. Let the recall of thoughts and incidents come and go. Just do not react and concentrate on the breath.

-Create stillness in the mind. Moreover, in that stillness plant the wish. When the wish is planted in still and calm mind, it manifests the best. In the free flow of energy, wishes receive incessant energy that enables them to manifest.

HOW DOES AFFIRMATION WORK?

'The reality shapes in mind.'

" Aham Brahma Asmi" is the only way to create reality in the mind. The vision suggests us that any form of constraint can be overcome through inner transformation.

For the achievement of an idea, one should extricate itself from object referral. Object referral is the need to get approval from outside. We should never let ourselves to be defined by external forces or by others.

Our definition of self is what we are really from inside, that can be achieved by raising the level of our awareness.

As it is suggested by Aristotle, **"The energy of the mind is the essence of life."**

Anything physical is the molecular blue print of energy or vibration. The physical world is the manifestation of the thoughts, the fine vibrations of our body. Thoughts have power to attract energy as the trees attract rain.

Make a wish box-using pyramid-

A pyramid due to its definite geographical shape receives energy better. Therefore it is recommended to put wishes written on a piece of paper in the pyramid.

Size of the paper to write wish

It is recommended to take paper of 7.7" and write the wish with red ink/ jells. It is to be kept in the Reiki pyramid after folding it to appropriate size.

Size of the pyramid:

Height	Base	Side
3"	4.71"	4.48"
4"	6.28"	5.98"
5"	7.47"	7.11"

The pyramid box can be made at home (using white cardboard) or it can be purchased.

ARPANA KUMAR

CHAPTER TWO

FIVE REIKI PERCEPTS

- JUST FOR TODAY, I WILL LET GO OF ANGER.
- JUST FOR TODAY, I WILL LET GO OF WORRY.
- JUST FOR TODAY, I WILL LIVE IN ATTITUDE OF GRATIDUE.
- JUST FOR TODAY, I WILL DO MY WORK HONESTLY.
- JUST FOR TODAY, I WILL LOVE AND BE KIND TO ALL LIVING BEINGS.

The word **today** gives impetus to **"Present Moment Awareness"** as in the present moment we sow the seed of future. Taking care of present moment ensures healthy future.

First Degree Reiki helps us to control the mind. After stepping in Reiki, the adept is expected not to be judgmental. It teaches us to be observant of our behavior. Being non-judgmental and observant helps us to travel the path of life blissfully. It also saves our precious life force energy that can be fruitfully used to better the self.

Meditation helps us to provide perfect ground to it. During meditation five percepts of Reiki help to build it, further.

The five percepts of Reiki prepare groundwork for healing. It opens the path of supreme healing and source of life force energy. The spiritual healing releases the adept from karmic bondage, illness and sufferings.

Buddhist description of five Percepts of Reiki.

The five Reiki percepts are meant to facilitate us the life force energy. Acting as the passwords to remove the blockade, it enables the adept to receive the life force energy in totality. The blockades present inside us are inhibitions, indecision and negative attitudes. They also hinder relationships.

How do the Reiki Percepts work for us?

I won't anger and won't worry- the affirmation is done on physical level but its response reaches to conscious and then subconscious level. It helps the adept to work on outward response.

These two percepts are designed to reach both "ego" and "intellect." Intellect stores information of the past and present. Based on these informations it takes decision for future. Whereas ego is the mask, the role one is playing in life. It often restricts the person.

The ego and intellect are carried from one body to another, one life to another as soul.

Healing of ego keeps it in the limit. It also gives perception to the adept about the futility of identifications as it restricts one. The percept also works on intellect. It gives clarity to perception that leads us to take better decision in the life.

I would earn my living with honesty and **I would honor my parents, elder and teachers.**-The percepts work on mental and emotional level.

The mind works through the senses. Based on like and dislike of senses sometimes the mind takes control of the body and ruins it. Because it dictates to body to do what is pleasurable and push aside what is not. Pushed by like or dislike it often manifests as indulgence or addiction.

Healing at mental level and Manomaya Kosh gives clarity and better perception to the senses. It gives awareness to changes around us and reasons to understand the ever-fleeting nature of it. Acquired awareness gives the senses better response.

I would show my gratitude to all living beings- Itworks on the spiritual level. It is the combination of both our inner and outward worlds.

One achieves the state of gratitude when the other levels (mind and ego, intellect or soul) are healed.

It is designed to reach the mind and **"ego, intellect and soul."** After that one connects self to cosmic level or move towards enlightenment.

The percept heals ego and intellect or the mental level/ mind and Manomaya kosh or aura. While healing the soul it takes care of Vigyanmaya Kosh where soul resides and in turn takes care of the past and present karma.

How do Reiki Percepts heal ?

Place the hands over the face and affirm, "Just for today I won't anger.

Anger comes when we feel threatened. Our preparations seem short of the imposing circumstances.

It also points us about our wrong breathing habits. Distortion in breathing comes when emotions are not balanced. Lower emotion of anger and jealousy upsets the harmony of breath. Thus, normal sequence of breath- pause, inhalation, pause, exhalation becomes disoriented. Therefore, the breath is to be harmonized.

To heal the percept we place our hands on temples and say, **"Just for today do not worry."** The temples are related to the balance of the passive and active sides of the brain, therefore using this principle here indicates balance of thoughts and thinking.

The Right hemisphere controls emotional issues whereas the Left hemisphere is analytical and logical. Whenever one side becomes overactive, worry starts. Thus healing both the hemispheres with the percept serves the purpose the best.

Placing our hands over the back of our head, say "I would honor my parents, elders and teachers." The back brain is the place where the memories of subconscious brain reside. As they are buried there unutilized, thus after some time they start blocking the fresh thoughts and ideas.

Healing of the back brain clears the junks of the brain that gives way to fresh workable idea. The subconscious brain stores past memories which we need to discard time to time.

The discarded junk gives way to strengthen and heal our original relations and dealing with the elders, teachers and parents.

Thus, the percept **"I would earn my living honestly"** must be reaffirmed putting the hands on Throat Chakra,

This is the area of communication. Communication helps us to interact with outer world. Our living depends enough on our communication to outer world.

Throat is also the area where thyroid gland is present. Thyroid gland is responsible for metabolism and for physical and mental strength. Earning and living of a person depends accordingly on physical and mental strength.

For healing heart chakra and gratitude we should reaffirm the percept, **"I would show my gratitude to all living beings."** TheHeart is the chakra of love and gratitude.

The reaffirmation of the percepts goes deep into sub-conscious. Thus, it heals the emotions, mental attitudes and relationships.

Healing of the Heart chakra with the Reiki Percepts aligns the other upper and lower chakras as well. The upper chakras are Crown, Third Eye Chakra, Throat Chakra and lower chakras are Solar plexus, Hara Chakra and Root chakra.

Illumination happens when the percepts become an ingrained nature of self. And at a point it ingrains in the sub conscious. The balanced Heart chakra brings the highest emotions of joy, love and gratitude. The energy of the highest emotion opens doors to health, wealth and prosperity.

The Buddhist belief says that the **three Klesha of life are main obstacles** like **hate, craving and ignorance.** They prevent us from ascending to spiritual path. The five percepts help us to heal and transcend these negativities.

Healing Buddha and Effect of Healing

According to Shington Buddhism, Vajrayana Mandala of Medicine Buddha comprises of five Buddha or Tathagat that are of different colors and represents different directions.

The five percepts of Reiki are the keys to receive life force energy from different directions.

The Buddha or Tathagat of different directions are Aksobhya, Amitabha, Amogasiddha, Ratnasambhava and Vairocana.

These Buddha are the Lords of different directions through which we receive life force energy. The different directions also represent different zones of our lives.

East- wood/elders -**Buddha Aksobhya**

West- earth/ material possessions- **Buddha Amitabha**

North- water/ career- **Buddha-Amogasiddha**

South- fire/ fame - **Buddha Ratnasambhava** At the centre – represents soul-**Vairocana**

Esoteric association of Healing Mandala

Buddha	Family	Color/Element/Symbolism	Direction/Wisdom/Posture	Cause/Result	Season	Wisdom
Vairocana	Buddha	White/Space/Wheel	Centre/Accomodating/Dharma Teaching	Wheel of Dharma/Ignorance/Delusion	Transition period	Wisdom of Dharma
Amogh Siddhi	Karma	Green/Air/Visvavajra	North/Accomplishment/concept/fearlessness	Protection, destruction /jealousy	Spring	Wisdom of perfection
Amitabha	Lotus	Red/fire/lotus	West/Inquisitive/perception/meditation	Attachment /selfishness, lust	Summer	Wisdom of observation
Ratnasambhava	Jewel	Gold, yellow/earth/jewel	South/equanimous/feeling/giving	Enrich. Increase/pride, greed	Autumn	Wisdom of Equanimity
Aksobhya	Vajra	Blue/water/vajra	East/non dualist/humility	Pacify, accept/aggression, aversion	Winter	Wisdom of reflection

Explanations of percepts

"Just for today," enables one to stay in present moment awareness.

Just for today I won't do anger - (Buddha Aksobhya)

Buddha Aksobhya – The imperturbable Buddha teaches us not to get angry. Reiki healing strengthens the person. The acquired strength enables a person to handle circumstances without getting panicked. It suggests that Reiki healing enables the adept to acquire the Buddha Aksobhya.

Awareness to anger helps to identify out trigger point or the cause. Anger feeds on precious life force energy. It drags one in foul mood and makes weary. Nothing can be accomplished in foul mood and low energy. Anger is a poison that kills self and weakens our efforts. It destroys all the virtues of a person.

Cause of anger- being insulted, intense disappointment, feeling vulnerable or threatened.

Cure- politely communicate your norms and expectations without blaming other people.

Just for today I won't worry—(Buddha Ratnasambhava)-

The Buddha Ratnasambhava-The Buddha of compassion also known as Buddha of abundance. Abundance or prosperity stays in peace. Worry always dispels peace.

Abundance is maintained only when the exchange happens. In better economy money rolls, in the same way for abundance we must give or take.

However, worry checks the flow as it dwells persistently in fear and insecurity. The created blur makes the person insecure and indecisive.

Insecure and indecisive mind pushes abundance away from a person's life.

Indecisiveness is always accompanied with worry. Thus wrapped in gloom, one makes wrong decisions in the life.

Calmness brings abundance in the life. Nevertheless, it takes a great deal of awareness and diligence in our part to stop worry and induce peace.

A way to deal with anger or worry is to find its source- tension or stress in the body.

Reiki helps to remove the stress.

Cause of worry- feeling of uncertainties and lack of courage. Moreover, our inability to take risks causes worry. On the other hand, often lack of preparation or readiness causes worry.

Cure- One shouldvisualize himself doing what he wants to do. Doing affirmation everyday helps to build the self-confidence and prepare groundwork for solution.

Worry is like a rocking chair; it gives us something to do; but gets us nowhere. -Van Wilder.

Just for today I would honor my parents, teachers and elders- _(Buddha Amitabha)_-

Honoring the people is only possible when one stays in higher self.

Honoring the elders helps us to stay in higher self persistently.

Buddha Amitabha- the Buddha of infinite light is the personification of compassion and represents the higher self.

Amitabha forgives everyone sins- a most appropriate quality to ascend the higher self but most difficult feat to achieve.

The percept heals our relationship and attitude with our parents, teachers and elders. When the elderly zone of life is unhealed, it often crops up in life as problematic relationship with elderly or when we take the role of mentor or parents. Healed attitude serves the best while dealing with both roles.

To have a content life we need to address our archetype as our relationships and outcome of efforts are based upon them.

Teachers and elders also represent our role as learners. In day to day dealing with the outer world we are constantly either receiving or giving suggestion to others. Thus, acknowledgement to our archetypes is essential.

If in our lives, we are unable to manage relationships as learners and teachers, it reflects on the quality of our lives. These issues cannot be ignored for long.

Showing respect and gratitude is the right way to deal with them.

Sometimes due to certain reasons, one finds it difficult. Some find it even more difficult while citing relevant or valid reasons. Even if the elders are difficult people they deserve our gratitude and respect. One can do it clarifying his or her stand politely.

For some of us it is the hardest thing to do. Only with this attitude, one can retain gratitude in his/her life.

The emotion of gratitude opens the Heart chakra and subsequently it also balances the upper chakras and lower chakras. The emotions of gratitude bring abundance, health and prosperity in our lives.

Goodness first strengthens and benefits the self then it reaches to people around us.

When we honor and acknowledge any one or elders, we transcend to our higher self every time. Therefore, this principle helps us to get in touch with our honorable self.

I would earn my living honestly- (Buddha-Amogasiddha)-

The north sector of Buddhist Mandala is the direction of water element and career. It is also the direction of mind and emotions.

For insights on directions, Vastu and Vedic knowledge also helps and works in the same way.

The Budda Amogasiddha personifies learning of life. He is also known as the "Buddha of infallible success." Working on earlier steps of Reiki percepts gives peace and focused state. In the focused state, our learning can be best utilized for the best earning.

For instance to write a book, knowledge is important. However, knowledge without clarity and focused approach cannot bring forth completion of the book.

Budda Amogasiddha is that state of one's self which realizes the true potential of one's learning. Moreover, acknowledging him in our lives we can focus our learning and potential for the best of our earning.

I would show gratitude to all living beings. _(Buddha Vairocana)_

The Buddha Vairocana, symbolizes the great Sun and our soul. Buddhist thoughts as well as Vedic wisdom suggest that Buddha Vairocana/ great Sun/our soul is the innermost layer of our Aura or existence. Thus in Mandal Buddha Vairocana who represents our soul stays at the middle of the Mandala.

Our soul travels from one birth to other and it carries past and present karma. The past and present karma controls our lives. The chronic diseases are said to be reason for unhealed soul or past karma.

Therefore in Vedic as well as in Buddhist thoughts it is recommended to do regular rituals and worship to cleanse souls.

As chronic illness takes more time to manifest or in getting cured, in the same way healing of the soul takes longer time. Therefore, it is the best to do the healing of the soul and karma on regular basis.

During healing and meditation session, the body stops producing cortisol and adrenaline (Flight and Flight hormone) that prepares body to handle the emergency by increasing heartbeat and dilating pupils. Instead, it enhances production of Immune boosting endorphin that relieves pain, reduces stress and improves mood.

We see in certain parts of our country when the Sun changes its position from southern horizon to northern or vice- versa during spring and autumn; worship of the Sun is under taken.

Such worship helps to restore the weak receiving of life force energy.

Vairocana is the Buddha of gratitude, the highest energy can be reached only after the working on the qualities of the previous four Buddha. To acquire gratitude we need to heal other emotions of mind.

All other four percepts of Reiki are the pathways to gratitude.

Healing anger calms the mind. Calm mind gives clarity and focus. Focus and concentration lead to wisdom that manifests in the life as better decisions and better career. Focus and concentration lead to wisdom, in fact enable us to show gratitude to everyone, whereas in anger and worry, we cannot show gratitude.

Thus to stay in gratitude to all beings we need to heal other four percepts of Reiki. At the same time practicing gratitude, helps us to heal all other four percepts of Reiki.

The first four principles are the steps designed to lead us to a point where the fifth principle becomes easier to accept and do.

Gratitude unlocks the fullness of life. Whatever we focus our attention at, it tends to grow. When we acknowledge gratitude in life, we increase the moment of highest self. In addition, at a point of time these increased moments of gratitude allow us to stay permanently in gratitude.

The mental attitude of gratitude unlocks the fullness of life to us. Gratitude turns what we have enough in more. It turns denial into acceptance, chaos into order and confusion in clarity.

CHAPTER THREE

CONCEPTS OF CHAKRAS

Chakras- *the energy wheel of spiritual body*

Chakras are the subtle energy centers on the spine. As an energy wheel on the subtle body, it receives the energetic vibrations of the universe. For sustenance, the corresponding organs and body use the absorbed life force energy.

Blockade in chakras, consequently blocks the intake of universal energy by body organs. So that healing of chakras is the key point for good mental and physical health.

How do emotions or negativities affect the chakras and physiology of the body ?

In the hierarchy of healing, emotions must be addressed or healed first. Emotions also show the energy level of a person. Therefore, emotions can be viewed as a barometer to see the level of energy inside the body.

Negative emotions such as hate, anger, indecision etc stay at low level of energy. At the low level of energy, the individual tends to yield to reactions. Consequently, he further dissipates the energy that manifests as the foul mood.

The vicious cycle of dissipation of energy leaves one fatigued and makes him sulky. In the long term, the sulkiness or negative emotions affect the organs and the physiology of the body. It can ultimately manifest as illnesses.

Number of chakras in the human body- There are 360 chakras in the body. The Primary Chakras are present on the spine whereas Secondary Chakras are present at the palm, knee, ankle and sole. Tertiary Chakras are present at the tips of fingers and toes.

Above the Crown chakra there are 745 cosmic chakras. With seven primary chakras at the spine and 745 cosmic chakras make total of 752. For eternal spiritual realization, it is believed that theses 752 chakras must be healed and aligned. It gives higher insights and perceptions of consciousness of the truth and eternal spiritual realities.

Therefore, the healing of 752 chakras is believed to be the minimum realization of the complete divine.

Crown chakra –The Crown chakra is 1000 petaled lotus. It is also known as Brahma Randhra/opening.

Third eye chakra is bi-petaled Bindu lotus or Ajna lotus in the middle of the forehead- one petal is towards right and other is towards left.

Throat chakra or the Vishuddha chakra is 16 petaled lotus.

Heart chakra is 12 petaled lotus. It is also called Sun lotus, the golden lotus, or the blossom of the day.

Solar plexus chakra is ten petaled lotus. Solar plexus is a complex of ganglia and radiating nerves of the sympathetic system at the pit of the stomach.

Hara chakra or Svadishtana chakra is six petaled lotus of bright red color.

Root chakra or Muladhara chakra lotus is four petaled of golden color.

Chakra and its Attributes:

Name	Position	Functions	Limbic functions	Sense	Element	Color	Seat	Kosh or aura layer	World/ region	Illness
Crown Chakra or Sahasrara chakra	Crown of head, right and left hemi sphere	Pineal gland	Divinity, peace, en-lightenment	Beyond senses or supra sen-sory	Ether or space	Violet	Libera-tion, eter-nal bliss	Not much in-formation about the layer	Satyam/ truth	Edema, ill-ness of res-piratory sys-tem
Third Eye Chakra or Ajna.	Between the eye-brows	Pituitary gland	Intuition, extra sensory perception	Sixth sense	Ether or space	Indigo	Primor-dial power	Not much in-formation on about layer.	Tapah/ pen-ance	Edema, illness of respiratory system
Throat Chakra or Vishud ha	Laryn-geal plexus	Thyroid	Self-expres-sion, speech	Hearing	Ether or space	Blue	Expression, communica-tion	Anandmaya	Janah	Boil, tumor, eyes diseases
Heart Chakra or Anaha ta	Thoracic region	Thymus, lungs	Compassion, love, healing	Touch	Air	Green	Love	Vigyanmaya	Mahah	Epilepsy, asthma
Solar Plexus Chakra or Manipura	Navel region	Pancreas, ab-dominal or-gans	Self- will, mental acu-ity, sense of identity	Sight	Fire	Yellow	Past and Subcon-scious emotion, ego, will	Maonamya	Savah/be-yond atmos-phere/cuasal	Asthma, ar-thritis, weakness of bones
Sacral Chakra or Swadhisth ana	Genitals, fluids	Gonads, re-productive organs	Self- ac-ceptance, emotions, sexual en-ergy	Taste	Water	Orange	Creativity	Pranamya	Bhuvah/ at-mos-phere/subtle	Insomnia, stones
Root Chakra or Mu-ladhara	Base of spine, sacral plexus	Excretory organs, adrenals	Survival, primal instinct	Smell	Earth	Red	Primal life force	Annamaya	Bhu/earth/ gross	Constipa-tion, diarro-hea, vomiting

CHAPTER FOUR

DIFFERENT LAYERS OF AURA AND ITS ROLE IN TOTAL WELL-BEING AND HEALTH

How does knowledge of aura serve the best?

The knowledge of aura layers helps in eliminating illnesses. Aura is the subtle sheath which covers the body. There are seven layers of aura.

Functions-

Each layer of aura is connected to different chakras of the body. Through the aura layer chakras receives universal energy. Subsequently chakras pump the energy into organs.

Whenever energy level of body falls, it first affects the aura layer. Thus in the energy healing system, aura is cleaned first.

The way to clean/ heal aura-

-By sweeping the body by Reiki energy.

-By joysticks/ agarbatti- move lighted joystick all around the person and in all directions of the room.

-By placing a saline (salt+water) water mug in the room, after six to eight hours, it should be discarded in the drain. Saline water has the power to absorb negativities.

Regular cleaning of aura layer heals or facilitates the healing faster.

Acknowledging the position of layers and guiding it for our benefits provides great help in healing.

Knowledge of different layers of aura gives insight about the chakras and organs. Thus during healing, it helps to address the root of illness and facilitates healing.

AURA OR BIOPLASMIC BODY SHEATH- A brief introduction.

Thousands of years ago, the ancient Ayurvedic Science identified —subtle energy sheaths around the body called aura or Bioplasmic Body.

-It is the thermo electric field or Aura which emanates from all matters, living or nonliving.

-The word 'Bio Plasmic comes from "plasma" which is the fourth state of the matter, the first three are- solid, liquid, and gas.

Aura layers are inter-permeable-

-The different layers of Aura have connectivity among them and each influences the other.

-The seven subtle sheaths of Aura are connected to seven chakras (subtle energy wheels) respectively.

-While covering the body as a sheath it receives universal energy from the Universe. It pumps energy to chakras of the body.

-Each aura layer is associated with definite color like chakras.

-Chakra is the bunch of ganglions and is the seat of important gland of the body.

Aura acts as a barometer of our health. Aura receives universal energy and pumps it into the Charkas. Theses are also the seats of specific glands of the body. The secretion of these glands controls the functions of the vital body organs.

Any disruptions of energy in the body, first spoils the aura, then the organs. The disturbances in energy flow breaks aura layer and energy dissipates through the holes. It also pollutes its color. Therefore, in healing, aura should be healed first.

FIVE IMPORTANT AURA LAYERS OR BODY SHEATHS

1. Anadamaya Kosh (The Blissful layer is the Sheath of Self) –

It is the innermost sheath. It is made up of five layers. The human consciousness is present at the center of the Kosh. The blissful, innermost layer is our real self, the original one.

-The kosha is also known as Hiranyamaya kosh, Hridaya kosh, Hridaya guha, Ling sharir, Causal body etc.

-Its location is in the heart and has close relation with our inner world. The existence of our gross body and our relation with the world is dependent on it.

To realize the state of bliss, objection less meditation or Nirbija Samadhi helps. Once the state is acquired, the seeker becomes free of the shackles of physical life and enjoys a blissful condition.

It is the kosh of soul, thus it travels from one birth to another. In the course, it accumulates the past lives experience and obstructions.

Self is truth and the truth never changes. It tells us to uncover our true self and to discard blur. So grounded in strength of self, one can sail the life successfully. The pristine self never changes, only its surrounding i.e. the body is subject of change.

The Blissful Kosh or Causal Body or Layer of Soul tells us the purpose of our existence on the earth. Each of us is on the earth with certain purpose.

Usually wrapped in ambiguity, many of us fail to see within. Thus, we live purposeless life for the sake of living. Moreover, our real talents and potential remain buried inside.

Often people follow norms set by the society that are considered fashionable as they lack clarity about their own potential.

The layer can be awakened to gain clarity about our goal and potentials. On this layer of the field, the soul's plan for lifetime is found.

Religious teaching of reincarnation or transmigration of souls suggests that in multiple lifetime the soul transcend and evolve. Besides, we make the mistakes and incur karmic lessons or debts in every lifetime.

All the love, knowledge and karmic lessons are source that determine our existence or life form on the earth. They act as a source of our birth. In addition, they replicate the consciousness to those particular life forms.

The physical body perfectly replicates the consciousness of the being within it. It serves to manifest in physical form all the abilities and lessons that each individual soul wishes to experience, express and learn. All such information about one's individual lifetime as well his all previous life times is contained with the causal body or on the soul.

2. Vigyanmaya Kosh or Sheath of Ego and Intellect- made up of five sheaths, it is the **sheath of knowledge.** It is made up of ego and intellect, the preceptor or the mind. Together they constitute the psyche.

"Ego" is the mask of ours, the role one plays in the universe. It is not our real self. Ego always works on fear and appreciation. Desire is fuel of it.

Intellect is the storehouse of environmental information that it carries as the genetic information. It carries the information of past, present and anticipates future.

The intellect gets input of surroundings through its senses and thus dependent on senses it creates dualities, for instance - like and dislike. It gives the feeling of pain and pleasures and emotions like love and hate.

While knowing the nature and functions of the Kosh one can modulate the thoughts and can act accordingly to keep himself away from illusions, worldly temptations, attachment etc.

Detachment with worldly temptations and instilling the stillness with Dhyana and Samadhi one can achieve the highest state of wisdom. It alienates one from falsehood, illusion, unsteadiness and other negative qualities.

This layer is also known as Astral Body or layer of Para-Conscious. It is the layer of intuition, extra sensory perception, image projection and spiritual sight.

Intuition empowers the person to connect with another person. Intuition helps a person to catch and decipher the subtle vibrations of the Universe. These subtle vibrations are always present around us but lost in blur, we are not able to perceive it.

HARNESSING AND WORKING ON THIS AURA MAKES A PERSON INTUITIVE. An intuitive person can connect with the aura of other person and can feel and understand vibrations of the universe.

The healed, healthy layer of aura when opens, one experiences that unity with others. The healed aura connects him to the information that is passing constantly through the cosmos.

3. Manomaya Kosh (Mental body layer- the preceptor)-

It is the prime body layer that guides the functions of Annamaya and Pranmaya kosh.

It is the layer of conscience where reasoning, feeling and emotions are felt.

The conscience or antahkarana chatushtaya is made up of mind, intelligence, ego and chitta.

It guides the five sense organs (eyes, ears, nose, tongue and skin). It makes us aware to external world through the sense organs.

Mind is the tool of consciousness. As a tool, it perceives the world and process information.

The mind makes perception through senses. Mind collaborates past experiences for perception and then creates duality in mind, for instance, happiness and sorrow, like and dislike. Thus duality of mind is due to senses.

Entangled in obscured facts of past, sometimes it loses opportunities and growth. Further, in the active mind sometimes "ego" dominants. Ego works on the fuel of desires. More will be the desire and attainment; more enhanced would be the ego.

In different births of life, ego, mind/ intellect and self, together of three out of five kasha travel from one body to another from one life to another.

In human body, mind works through brain whereas in lower animal mind works through the perception of their body cells. Thus, mind is present in every cell of the body.

Functions

a. The layer also controls intellectual functions, our conscious and unconscious mind and memories. The conscious mind refers to those aspects and environment we are aware of. Unconscious thoughts are the past experience that stays in subconscious brain.

b. The mental layer co-ordinates physiological activities of the body that include conscious and autonomic function.

For instance, driving a car is a conscious effort whereas skill of diving is stored in subconscious brain. Thus, the subconscious skill which is monitoring the present moment enables a person to drive without thinking about it.

c. The subconscious is the site of past memory. It keeps past memories in the cells of body organs. The past memories drive the required organs to work and act as habit.

However, the long untended subconscious creates distraction and steals focus. In the long run, it causes ailments like insomnia etc. It also distracts a person from "living in now."

The present moment awareness gives concentration and clarity, enables one to percept right, and take right decisions. It is a productive way of living with success.

The unexamined ideas, believes, judgments and concepts are junks of brain. They unnecessarily occupy memory space.

Thus, they should be discarded at the earliest. They block the circulation of energy in the field. They stand rigidly on the way to new information and create ambiguity to the perception.

The ambiguities are the knots of negativities. They stay in the muscles as tension. They block circulation of energy within the field and prevent new information and understanding of life.

In Reiki sessions when these knots are released, the creativity emerges and flexibility is felt. The blocked energy prevents one from seeing the opportunities and possibilities.

4. Pranmaya Kosh/ Pranic body/ Etheric body (life sustaining health energy layer or vital air)- the seven layers of Aura or Kosh collectively called Pranmaya Kosh.

It is the body between gross and physical body. It permeates through the Annamaya kosh.

It acquires knowledge for the physical body and directs the functions of the physical body.

It also functions as a medium through which we enjoy the pleasures derived from the functioning of the sense organs and mental processes.

By regular practice of Pranayama and Reiki healing the Pranmaya Kosh becomes more energetic and efficient which in turn energizes the Annamaya Kosh or Kosh of physical body.

It supplies vital air to the whole body that keeps it alive. Breath is physical counterpart of the mind. In a mechanical way breath enables the life force energy to feed neuro-motor and sensory activities of body.

Breath has power to control the mind and vice versa.

5. Annamaya Kosh (Sheath of matter)- it is the main center of physical body. The last of five kosh are found in the brain and on the spine. The cerebro spinal system is the first part of the organism to be developed after conception. From it, the entire body comes out.

The functioning of the body system is controlled by spine and the Psychic center is located on it.

It begins from the skin of the body and reaches the inner recesses such as Bones, flesh, all organs, brain etc. It is related to the element of earth and is indicated by density. Purity of food, proficiency of asana and Pranayama render it clean and healthy.

The Annamaya kosh or etheric body has direct connection with the physical body- cells, tissues and organs. It is infused with the ovum of etheric body.

The breadth of it extends between two to five inches from the body. It is often referred as etheric double as all organs are replication of etheric form. In another word, the entire body is a physical manifestation of the etheric body.

CHAPTER FIVE

BUDDHIST CONCEPT OF HEALING METHODS

Buddhist concepts of illness-

Buddhist thought suggests that the "dualities" and "ego" are the cause of disharmony. Duality creates like and dislike, which is an energy dissipating process. The vicious cycle of duality dissipates energy and under weariness, the person frequently yields to reactions.

On physical level, balance or imbalance of energy level is responsible for health and diseases.

Acknowledgement of the dissipation of energy level and willingness to control it helps the best. Wisdom and knowledge is the panacea of all ailments.

According to Buddhist concept three Klesha (Confusion, Attachment and Aversion) are the real cause of mental and physical ailment. These three klesha cause three dosh or illnesses in the body namely Wind/ Vayu, Bile/ Fire/Pitta and Phelgm/ Kapha.

The cause of mental and physical ailments are-

Confusion- It is caused by the ignorance- **Kapha imbalance.**

Attachment- It is caused by craving and indulgence-**Vayu** imbalance.

Aversion- It is caused by hate -**a Pitta imbalance.**

Noble cures of Buddha-

Wisdom cures **ignorance**- It is produced due to desire and hatred.

Morality cures desire, greed and lust.

Concentration and **calmness** cure anger, hatred and repulsion.

What do the three Klesha (three primary emotions) point us ?

Body is of elemental nature (made up of Punchbhutas- earth, water, fire, air and ether).

The disharmony of Punchbhutas creates obscuration or further disharmony in three body humeral (Vayu, Pitta and Kapha)

Note – The three body humeral arise due to disharmony or faults of Punchbhutas (or elements of the body).

The three Klesha	Creates imbalance in body constitution as Vayu, Pitta and Kalpha	Diseases and aggravations it produces in body.	Reason	Associated chakras	Associated deities and planets
Confusion	Kalpha (disharmony of water and earth)	Diabetes, fatigue etc.	Ignorance Cure - lies in shedding passivity by exercise and other methods.	Root and Ham Chakra	Mercury (earth)- Lord Ganesha, Venus and the Moon. Devi worship(Ma Gauri, Ma Lakshmi and Ma Saraswati)
Attachment	Vayu (disharmony of air and water)	Racy brain, mental disorders, restlessness, dry skin and hair.	Craving and indulgence. Cure – practicing calmness with meditation and chanting mantra	Head, Crown, Third Eye, Root Chakra (as physical body houses mind).	Jupiter (ether/ space)-Lord Buddha, Saturn (air) - planet Saturn, Lord Hanuman, Lord Shiva.
Aversion	Pitta (disharmony of fire and earth)	Blood pressure, heart disease	Hate or lack of love Cure- create more love and self-respect in life.	Heart chakra.	Mercury (earth) - Lord Ganesha.

FIRST DEGREE REIKI MANDALA- It is Buddhist Yantra or energy pattern which tells us about the hierarchy of healing. At the first Degree Reiki Mandala, there are 12 Yaksha General (time) and 10 directions (place).

The 12 Yaksha General (time) and Gods of ten directions (place) ensure one being in the right place at the right time.

The First degree Reiki Mandal works at the physical level.

At First Degree Mandala there is **Yaksha/General (time)(represent parts of our brain which control or are responsible for that body part).** It has a PRIMEVAL OR BASIC or animal associate who represents our body parts. It shows that within us both human and animal instincts exist.

In vedic scripture of HINDU PANTHEON of the God (the energy pattern or the deity) that represents highest self of existence has an animal counter part that is also known as wahan or mount or vehicle of that particular deity. The animal counter part represents lower self of the existence.

In astrology also, all ten direstions are connected with certain planets and represented by certain deities and show their elmental characterteristics.

Now, back to REIKI MANDALA explanation, Yaksha, the Guard demands certain healed aspect of ours before allowing to reach the guardians. The guardians are the Gods of ten directions. The guardians of ten directions represent different zones of our lives. Through ten directions we receive life force energy in our lives.

Direction	Zone of life	element
East	Elder/mentor/ superior	Wood
South east	Wealth	Wood
South	Fame/power/ status	Fire
South west	Marriage	Earth
West	Creativity/Finance creation/Progeny	Metal
North west	Helpful people/ friends	Metal
North	Career	Water
North west	Knowledge/ education	Earth
Above	Sky	Space
Down	Earth	Earth

The First Degree Reiki heals the first level of Reiki Mandala. Thus it enables the adept to receive blessings from all directions.

The God of ten directions also represents the different elements or tattva of the body. The First Degree Reiki heals the different tattva or constitution and humeral of body. It manifests as good health.

The GUARD or Yaksha represents parts of our brain or our EMOTIONS which block receiving.

The Yaksha Generals indicate human awareness or the state of higher self. Higher self stays with us in harmonious state. While their animal associates represent our basic animal instinct- a state of lower energy. In lower energy we yield to reactions.

In fact, the world of matter is vibratory in nature. In the vibratory world all matter particles, animate of inanimate are vibrating at certain level of energy. We, human have consciousness-mind and intellect, which give perception of emotions. The nature of emotions is dependent on level of energy as well.

When we are stressed, the energy level falls. And in lower energy, emotions like anger, irritation and jealousy make their way in thoughts. The state is called foul mood.

When we elevate the energy level by rest, food, breathing exercise or Reiki healing we acquire higher level of energy and our thought patterns acquire positive emotions of love and joy. That we usually refer as good mood.

Life is a choice. When we acknowledge the ever-changing state of our mind and emotions, we apply efforts to mend it. Otherwise, many of us wrapped in ignorance perennially sulk. In unawareness, we always point the origin of bad mood outside.

The Doorman or Yaksha/ General represents our –true self, innate nature, talent and potential.

The guardians of ten directions (positive aspects of ours) represent our relationships. It has a female partner (negative aspect of ours).

The guardians of ten directions point us to make the ground for proper receiving of life force energy from all ten directions.

Yoga as well as Buddhist thought prescribe groundwork for bliss as **right understanding, right efforts, right mindfulness, right speech, right action, right bodily action, right livelihood, right concentration, right conception-** they lead to wisdom and eventually to bliss.

Result: right time + right place+ wisdom= success or luck.

The guardians of ten directions represent our attitudes and inhibitions. It also acts as guard to our relationships. The guardians reflect the positive and negative aspects of people. These two attributes are present in every one of us.

Thus, First Degree Reiki is about healing our outer life and its impact on our body, which is reflected in our actions, reactions and relationships.

The nerve, endocrine, muscles and immune system carry the emotions in human being.

Developing our innate nature, practicing being non-judgmental and being observant of our behavior help to travel the path of healing and live the life successfully and blissfully.

CHAPTER SIX

WHAT ARE WE AS HUMAN BODY ?

The human body is made up of -

Five elements (ether, air, fire, water and earth).

Three humerals (Vayu, Pitta and Kapha)- They determine how the body treats food and air one breathes.

Five energies (Prana, Apana, Vyana, Sumana and Udana)-The five energies affect digestion and metabolism.

Ayurveda suggests that the gross or physical body is made up of saliva, blood, flesh, fat, bone, marrow and reproductive fluid.

Astrologically, body isgross or **physical body** (flesh and bone), **subtle body** (consciousness and emotions) and **causal body** (karna sharira or soul). On causal body exist the physical and subtle body.

Five Koshas or Aura layers- The three bodies operates in conjunction with five sheathes, the Kosha or Aura layers.

Annmaya Kosh (Kosh of Physical body)- is physical layer which is connected to root chakra.

Manomaya Kosh (Mind)- a sheathe which brings energy to mind. Mind is the tool that enables us to perceive the outer world through our senses.

Mind does the job of cognition, perception and understanding.

Pranamaya Kosh (Kosh of Breath)- is the layer of life. Prana energy in the form of breath permeates through all body organs.

Vigyanmaya Kosh (Ego and Intellect)- Intellect is the storehouse of past and present information. Whereas ego is the mask, the role we are playing in the world. We need to work through the intellect with complete awareness rooted in now and keeping ego at bay.

Anandmaya Kosh- is the blissful kosh.

The vedic wisdom says that the root of all illnesses arises from three klesha or misery. **The three klesha of human life is confusion, attachment and aversion.**

In life, confusion arises due to ignorance; attachment arises due to craving or uncontrolled desires. Desire is the evil of all ruins. Aversion arises due to hatred.

The **three klesha** or misery arise due to disharmony of **duality and ego**.

All education or Vidya of Buddhist as well as Vedic (Yoga, Ayurveda, Astrology, Worship, Tantra and Mantra) are centralized to work upon correcting the **body, mind and soul.**

CHAPTER SEVEN

HIERARCHY OF HEALING

Healing takes care of the body. A strategic healing serves better. It is thus pertinent to know what we are.

Hierarchy of Reiki healing-

Healing must be aimed at these bodies:

- Body- physical body
- Mind-subtle body
- Soul-causal body
- Kerna body- cosmic body

Taking care of all these bodies enables one to receive more energy.

Thus tending the physical body to heal first is the best way to start healing as it houses other fine bodies.

Steps to heal physical body-

Head-

- It is the center which controls body functioning.

-It is also biggest consumer of nutrients and oxygen (about 20 percent of total consumption of the body).

-It is the controller of thoughts and body physiology.

Front of the body-

Healing front part of the body takes care of the body organs. Front is also said what we create in our lives whereas back represents what we receive from destiny, relations and from our surroundings.

Back of the body-

Dorsally from our back, the spine passes. Through the spine the subtle body of chakras and meridian [**Ira** (Moon nadi), **Pingala** (Sun nadi) and **Sushumna** (central nadi)] pass.

Ira-Moon nadi (mind)-the Moon controls the mind.

Pingala – Sun nadi- Sun: It is the controller of body vitality and physiology. The Spine is also the place where the subtle body of all chakras is located. On chakras key glands of the body are located which manage vital physiology of the body, i.e. metabolism, excretion, reproduction etc.

So healing the back with Reiki energy takes care of spine, chakras and meridians.

CHAPTER EIGHT

IMPORTANCE OF CHAKRAS HEALING AND ITS EXPLANATIONS

The subtle energy wheels of the body chakras are also the seats of vital glands of the body- like pineal, pituitary, thyroid, adrenal, gonads etc. These glands control the vital functioning of the body like metabolism, reproduction, immune system, circadian cycle, emotions and body vitality. All primary chakras are present on the vital glands of body. Thus healing the chakras takes care of glands and their physiology.

Healing of **Root Chakra** is vital as it represents physical plane of the body. It houses other subtle bodies like mind, soul and cosmic body.

According to astrology it is Bharyasthan , place of spouse, partnership, contract etc. healing of root chakra strengthen these aspects of life also.

Next to it is **Hara chakra**- the **Emotional Chakra**. Emotions originate in mind. Healing Hara Chakra is like healing our thoughts and uplifting it from negative to positive.

In unhealed condition, thoughts are the biggest dissipater of energy and manipulator of uneven breath. A thought of anger, hate in a moment changes the rhythm of breath and makes it shallow and unsteady. It cuts supply of requisite nourishment and oxygen to vital organs of body, specially the brain. Thus it creates persistent fatigue.

According to astrology, position of Hara chakra represents Ripusthan, the place of enemy and unfavorable people and circumstances of life. The ruling planet of the region is Venus.

Explanation- It is the place of about seventy two thousands plexus of nerve ganglion. Therefore, the place is also called second brain of the body. Any kind of mental stress accumulates here and with time first appears as the pain in lumber region, then full fledged ailment comes in body organs of that region.

Every thought is the currency of energy/creation.

Every negative thought dissipates energy and every positive thought (emotions of bliss- joy, love and gratitude) have power to generate energy with compound interest.

Solar Plexus Chakra- It is the center of power, mastery over skills. According to astrology, it is also known as Sukhasthan- the place of progeny. Its location is above the naval. Hara Chakra and Solar Plexus together determine the physical vitality and receiving of life force energy and strength of human body. The ruling planet of Solar Plexus is the Sun.

Key point- to have best of vitality Solar Plexus and Hara chakra must be strengthened.

Heart Chakra-Thereafter comes **Heart Chakra,** also known as Shakti sthala of the body. Healing of it can be equated with getting Siddhi or appeasing Goddess of Shakti-Pith as it enables the adept to acquire emotions of bliss (joy, love and gratitude) which is the gateway of growth, prosperity and health.

Emotions of bliss can only be acquired provided all other chakras, i.e. all lower chakras and upper chakras are healed, balanced and aligned.

In this way for total well being, healing of all chakras is pertinent.

According to astrology it is Matristhan/ place of mother and all wordly things which nourish and support us i.e. the mother earth, house and the first mentor of life, the mother. Therefore while healing it on physical level, we must take care of all these relations of life - be it mother earth, mother and our house. The ruling planet of the place is Moon.

Throat Chakra- it is the place of Thyriod gland and Parathyriod gland, responsible of metabolism and calcium balance in blood and bones consecutively.

It is also the place of communication. It relates to our day to day dealings with the world. Communication also determines our earning and our self-presentation in the world.

Usually thyroid problems crop in the body of those who communicate less with the world. Communication does not meant being talkative. It is like conveying the self with our surrounding world in the most honest way. One can do it through constructive expressions like singing, writing or with honest dialogues.

According to astrology, it is the place of Dhansthan, place of finance and earning power, therefore our communication with the world must be appropriate to earn better. The ruling planet of the place is Mercury.

Third eye Chakra- It is the place of **pituitary gland**, the master gland, that controls functioning of all other glands of the body and **pineal gland** that controls circadian cycle of the body.

According to astrology, it is Lagnasthan, the place of self. It is the place of self which shows our personality, nature, complexion, health, appearance etc. The ruling planet of the place is Mars.

Healing of Nadis-

Nadis can be equated with rivers as they irrigate and nourishes earth and living beings respectively. Likewise through nadis the Prana or Life Force energy flows and it nourishes the material body. There are about seven pairs of Nadis that pass through the body intersecting it vertically.

CHAPTER NINE

SOME KEY CONCEPT ABOUT HEALING

Healing of emotions prepares body to acquire harmony.

Dhyana/Meditation- are the means to still the mind.

Dharna/Morality-As preparation of the soil is essential for healthy crop, Dharna or morality are essential for the harmonized mind.

Healing of body- Chakras are the energy centers of the body.

Nadis (Can be equated as river)-Through Nadis the Prana or Life Force energy flows. It nourishes the material body as the river does to the earth and living beings.

Importance of heart chakras and Hara Chakra- Both Chakras are Shaktipith of physical body as meridians originate from it.

Emotions of bliss- Joy, love and gratitude stay in Heart chakra. They are the currency of affluence.

Why healing of emotions are important?

Regular healing by Reiki is needed to conserve wastage of energy in the body. As exposed to the world, physical body is constantly responding to reactions. When response turns negative, it dissipates energy. Persistent loss of energy drags down the receiving of life force energy. Lower level of energy blocks wisdom in life. It further blocks wisdom, affluence, power of creation and prosperity in life.

CHAPTER TEN

HISTORY OF REIKI

RYO HO means healing method, therapy, remedy or USUI SYSTEM OF NATURAL HEALING

THE REIKI STORY- Reiki heals the body and illuminates the mind. Therefore, every sensei tries to inculcate the values and learning of Dr Usui system of Reiki to the learner. The Reiki story appealed many masters to visit in-depth of it to find bigger meaning of it. As seekers, we traditionally look to our scriptures of faith to find answers of our inquisitiveness. Therefore, by different masters, it was illustrated and explained differently according to their faiths and research of different doctrines. I would love to explain it according to my knowledge and faith.

Dr Usui's life (1865-1926)

Dr Mikao Usui, was born on 1865 in Japan. He belonged to a trader's family. From his early life he was inclined to healing methods. Thus, he learned oriental healing methods and studied Japanese and Chinese medicine. Later, to enrich his knowledge he learnt Allopathy from Missionary doctors.

Once under the attack of malaria, he got some divine vision in near coma state. He shared his vision with the father of his school friend, a mature Shington Buddhist and asked interpretation of it. He advised Usui to seek its meaning through spiritual path. He accepted him under his wing for spiritual guidance.

The two branches of Buddhist Tendai and Shingon Buddhist were founded in Japan in the 7th century. They were brought to Japan by sensei Shuichi and Kukai. They were trained in China by two Indians Buddhist Masters. It is believed that Dr Usui was the reincarnation of Kukai.

A person needed initiation to channel Reiki energy, but Dr Usui was simply able to do it by practice.

While Dr Usui was studying some ancient books, one day he came across a scripture, "THE TANTRA OF LIGHTNING FLASH." The text had a sutra empowered to heal the body and illuminate the mind. The texts were in Japanese annotations.

It had been brought to Japan by Kukai. At that time, there wasn't any living teacher acquainted with the healing method of Tantra as it was an ancient healing method of Hinduism.

Decided to decode the lost method of Tantra Healing, Dr Usui opted to meditation as per Buddhist believe. For that he chose Kuriyama hill outside Kyoto to meditate and fast. Reiki must be practiced after getting initiated by a Reiki sensei. But Dr Usui undertook it by practice as there was not any practicing teacher of it at that point of time. He is believed to be an incarnation of Kukai that is why he didn't need any initiation to practice it.

The texts of Tantric Healing revealed that Reiki First, Second, and Third Degrees were the first level of Tantric healing. According to Dr Usui's Reiki Healing Method, life force energy could be raised by calming the mind. In higher level of Tantra the healer would get direct energy.

As per documental evidence, to decode the "Lotus Sutra", Dr Usui visited different monasteries.

Monasteries, the place of worship would often have with ample collections of religious texts. Finally, Dr Usui's search brought him to a Zen monastery where he met an old Abbot. Abbot helped him and provided him the requisite texts of learning. He helped him as a guide. Ultimately, the dedication of Dr. Usui piloted to success with the help of the Abbot.

For years, Dr Usui studied scriptures in Japanese, Chinese and Sanskrit. Subsequently he got acquainted with the Oriental Philosophy of Reiki.

Then he found the Lotus Sutras in Sanskrit text and decided to decode it in practical way. In Lotus Sutra he found formula to contact higher self and acquire the gift of healing.

Dr Usui visit to the mountain- With guidance of Abbot, Dr Usui went to Kuriyama hill to meditate and chant as prescribed in Lotus Sutra. While starting his spiritual journey, he made resolve to himself that either he would decode it in his meditation or embrace death in his endeavor. He revealed his intention to Abbot and asked him to send someone to bring his body from the hill, in case of his failure.

He placed of 21 stones during meditation-On the Kuriyama Hill, he chose a cave near a stream to meditate. He kept 21 stones in front of him to keep track of the day and with resolve to discard non-working faith and believes so that his calm and focussed brain could lead to wisdom. After meditation of a day, he would throw away a stone. **It was his strategic way to discard unfavorable believes which had been obstructing the path of his enlightenment.**

Vision of light on the eastern sky-On the 21st day, just before dawn, Dr Usui saw a dazzling bright light on eastern sky. Out of fatigue or under the cover of meditative serenity he froze while watching the dashing light. It touched him on his forehead and then expanded around him. After a while he felt, it covered him completely.

Engulfed in divine light, in his subconscious state, he then viewed hundreds of colored bubbles that contained the meaning of symbols and information of healing power. In fact, he was viewing the different Buddha of Buddhist healing Mandala. Their subsequent appearances were messages to him.

The symbols were telling him to acquire enough wisdom to heal the body. Healing power needed wisdom of fine senses. Only the flawless faculties of human body acquire the power of self-

correction.

Negativity blocks the power of perception. It brings misery on the physical and mental body.

In negativities, Buddha and wisdom often remain buried inside. However, when we allow wisdom to prevail by conscious efforts by discarding negativities, health follows us naturally.

His return journey to Kuriyama Hill- Around midday Dr Usui gained his consciousness. Although he was starved for twenty one days, still he was feeling energized and refreshed. Recalling the happening of dawn, in jubilation he hurried down to hill to share the news of his success to Abbot.

In his rush to descend the hill, he hit his toe to a stone. Blood oozed out of the toes. To stop the blood he held his toe in his hand. To his amazement, the pain subsided and oozing blood stopped.

He thus tested his discovery how Reiki empowers with healing power of hands.

His dining at the foot of the hill- At the base of mountain he met the roadside innkeeper who invited him at his inn for food. Conventionally, in Japan the innkeeper would take it as good omen to serve food to monk after his return from meditation. Dr Usui accepted the invitation of innkeeper and sat at the desk for the food.

At the inn, the innkeeper's granddaughter was serving the food to the people. Due to toothache, the girl's face and jaws were swollen. The girl had tied a cloth around her face to lessen the pain and chill.

Seeing the girl in pain, Dr Usui asked the girl to heal her with his hands. Dr Usui's healing mitigated the pain of the girl and swelling of her face went away. HE CONFIRMED HIS HEALING POWER.

The innkeeper requested him to wait for the while so he could prepare digestible meal suitable for long starved stomach. But Dr Usui insisted to serve him whatever already prepared as he was feeling very hungry. The innkeeper was surprised with his request. He gave him normal food which was prepared for other customers. Usui had the normal food after giving Reiki to it.

Reiki can be given to food for better digestion.

Dr Usui returned to Zen Monastery- On his return to monastery, Dr Usui took bath, changed his cloth and addressed an audience. In the meeting, he discussed the gift of healing to masses. Then, he healed devotedly Abbot's arthritis.

He changed his cloth meant here he had changed his old non-working faith and habits.

Dr Usui visited to the beggar city- After discussion with Abbot, Dr. Usui decided to go to a city of beggars, as in his opinion, the gift of divine healing must be available to the downtrodden first.

A beggars' city was situated outside Kyoto where lepers were living. Mikao Usui went there and revealed his intention to their chief to cure the lepers and to teach them a dignified way of living. The cynical beggars' chief viewed his request with cynicism.

The mean beggar chief, in lieu of his teaching permitted him to stay there with only one time meal. He gave him a tiny shed to stay and tattered cloth to wear. **The mentality of beggar's chief represents the lower level of energy. Lower level of energy always manifests in one as skeptics and fears. In poor mentality, a person always share less.**

Dr Usui stayed there for seven years. He believed that healing of young people would be easier and result would be quicker. He believed ailments of old people built over long time would also take long time to get healed.

After healing the young lepers at beggars' city, Dr Usui would send them to the monastery to teach Reiki. Before sending them, he would give them a new name and clothes.

One day Dr Usui realized that he was seeing the same young men in the beggars' city. When he asked them, they showed their pessimism to Reiki teaching. They were finding begging easier than teaching Reiki.

Dr Usui's realization- exchange of energy for the efforts of Reiki-

Dr Usui realized wrong application of his efforts. He decided to analyze the way of application once again. He felt the need of some exchange for the effort of Reiki. For appreciation of gift he felt need of some energy exchange between the giver and receiver. It is also known as the law of nature. People do not appreciate things which they get free.

Vedanta philosophy, as well as the Buddhist tradition also advocated, "The law of giving and receiving."

Presentation of Reiki –Dr Usui felt that nothing in this world could be imposed on any one, even with the best of intention. Benefits could only be gained from willingness. Christianity also advocated, "When the student is ready the teacher appears." He understood his miss of application.

Afterward he decided to heal and initiate people with Reiki energy when they would show their willingness.

Dr Usui's walk with torch in hand- During day, with lit torch in his hand, Dr Usui would walk in alleys of Japan to attract attention of people. He would reason them to have more light from Reiki. His explanation of more light meant more receiving of health, wealth and bliss in life.

Lamp in the hand of Dr Usui symbolizes the Buddhist thoughts of Buddha Sakayamani. It was taught by him, "Be your lamp to yourself."

The Christians belief too support it, "Always walk with your own sunshine whatever the weather be outside."

The Vedic wisdom says, "Aham Brahma Asmi," it means we, our body is naturally ingrained with healing power or power of creation. Only we need to invoke that power within us in appropriate way with regular practice.

Then he started teaching the Reiki methods to those who were interested and would come to him. In this way Dr Mikao Usui gifted the world the divine healing method of Reiki.

Conclusion-

Reiki teaches us to integrate and balance our positive energy. Therefore, we can live blissfully and can stay centered in calm state naturally.

Otherwise, in disintegrated way one yields to irritation and skeptics that mind often experiences.

Reiki teaches us to heal ourselves and integrate our energy regularly, till the focused state of our being gets ingrained in us and become our natural state. The healed state makes us calm and helps us to harness the riches of life.

Dr Usui's Reiki Healing Method teaches us that life force energy can be raised by calming the mind.

Life history of Madam Hawayo Takata

After the marvelous revival of Reiki by Dr Usui, the time for its expansion to the world came with the birth of Hawayo Takata. In the year 1900, a new era of Reiki started at the Hawaii Island when the little angel was born at a humble peasant's house.

Birth of Hawayo

It was Christmas eve, at the break of dawn when the sun was at the horizon spreading its golden hues, a baby girl was born at the humble household of the plantation peasant. It was the house of a farmer, the dozed mother surging out of the labor pain, glanced at the bundle of joy and she was lovingly named Hawayo by family members after the newly created territory of Hawaii.

In 1900's the life at the island was full of hardship specially the household of peasants where masses were engaged in cultivation. To beat the day to day hardship, children had to work during summer to support their families. Hawayo was keen to learning and studying since her childhood. At the age of twelve, she was studying in a village school. Like other children of the village, she too had to work in plantation fields during summer with other children.

Hawayo was a small statured child of lean frame. Her fragile frame would feel extreme exhaustion while working at the sugarcane field. Sometime out of exhaustion and lagging far behind in the work, she would start crying. Other workers and children feeling pity for her plight would come forward to help her and would provide helping hands to her assigned agriculture job.

The supervisor of the field watched her exhaustion of hard physical work. Feeling pity for her, he decided to help her.

The end of vacation came as a big relief to Hawayo. On the last day when other children after completion of their works boarded the vehicle in the jubilation, Hawayo decided to say a prayer to the almighty. Sitting in the middle of the field she bent and prayed raising her arms to the sky. She prayed to the God at the open field to spare her from the hard physical work in future.

Discomfort of hard physical work and prayer of Hawayo at the field were already witnessed by the manager. Filled with empathy he visited her house and intimated her parents about her uneasiness to hard work.

Thus with family consent Hawayo decided to look for other job prospects.

Hawayo's working life

In subsequent year, fortunately she was asked by her school to assist children of first grade. Delighted she grabbed the offer at once with parental consent.

At school Hawayo had been paid weekly and more importantly she was spared with exhaustion of physical work.

In 1914, she visited a store on inauguration at Lihue. There she was asked to assist the work of soda fountain by a family-known employee. Hawayo assisted him diligently. She welcomed and served the guests whole day. Pleased with her soft skills, the store owner honored her with a job offer.

Hawayo' family was still living the life of hardships. Thus, her parents duly appreciated the new job offer. To ease the financial constraints Hawayo had been working continuously. She acquired two jobs. In which she would work at the store on Saturday and rest of the week at her boarding school.

After completion of her studies, she joined the work at store on permanent basis.

As she was still staying at her boarding school and was assisting the children as well. Balancing the two jobs in hand, she had hardly any leisure but she was content.

One day, a woman of affluent plantation family visited the store as a customer. Soft-spoken Hawayo entertained her at the store. She got pleased with her poised service and interaction.

Impressed with her soft working skills, she offered her a job at her place. The remuneration of new job was double of her present salary with added incentives of food, lodging and clothing.

Although the new job offer meant a distant move for Hawayo from her parent's place. However, hardships of the family made her interested in pay hike. Therefore, she accepted the offer. She promised the lady to visit her during her next vacation.

The place of her new job was magnificent. It was a big mansion with cottages, stable and out-houses for domestic and plantation workers.

Hawayo worked there for twenty-four years. In that duration, her career spiraled upwards. She managed successfully different hierarchies of commitments, that ranged from waitress to pantry girl and then she got promoted as house keeper.

Acknowledgment came to her sincere efforts and soon she was promoted as supervisor. The job as supervisor entailed her to supervise salaries of mansion's staffs.

Hawayo's marriage

Working as the supervisor at the plantation mansion, she got introduced to a young man- Saichi Takata. Later in a few years she got married to him. In next few years the union got blessed with two daughters.

Saichi Takata had a decent job. Apart from that he had been also serving an honorary position at the territorial governor. There he was serving sport activities at the club. For years, they lived a blissful conjugal life.

The came the twist of destiny, the blissful union of Hawayo and Saichi lasted short. At the age of thirty-four Saichi Takata left for heavenly abode. However, for past few years he had been getting predomination about his death due to his deteriorating health. Therefore, he tried to convince Hawayo to make plan for her life and daughters after his death.

As a wife Hawayo was finding it too difficult to discuss his death. Shaken in fear she prayed for his well-being and ignored to discuss the topic of death.

However, after disclosure of Saichi premonition about his death, in a few days he made his transition from the world at the young age of thirty four. Though she was devastated by the loss yet Hawayo fulfilled his desire according to her strength. Saichi Takata was an earnest husband and community man. So his departure from the world was felt as a big loss not only for Hawayo and children but also for their community.

Illnessess and hard ships of Madam Hawayo-

After Saichi's transition, Hawayo had to work hard to support her children. The involved hardships of sustenance and big loss of life wrecked her completely. After sometime the mental trauma started taking toll on her health. Unable to handle it for long in weak health, she underwent nervous breakdown.

At that point of time, engulfed in mental trauma, one by one her apprehensions started manifesting as full physical ailments. She got respiratory and abdominal ailments.

Earlier diagnosis of her persistent pain, revealed an abdominal tumor. For that she was recommended surgery.

However, the Doctors found her too weak to get operated. Nevertheless, Physicians made it clear that surgery was inevitable. She had to regain her health to work and support her family.

Hawayo was an Oriental Buddhist. To respite her exhausted self she would often meditate. In her meditation, she would try to find answers to her problems. Prioritizing her responsibilities, she would try to get way out from her problems. Health was her prime concern. As to support her family at every cost, she had to restore it. So reverently, she would sit for meditation and seek help from the almighty.

Already she had been anguished but there were more pains in store in her destiny . She lost her sister in very short illness. Hawayo was the one who had been staying with her. Thus, she had to deliver the distressing news of her demise to her parents. The incident shook her from the core.

Unable to handle more troubles, for some respite she visited her parents' place in Japan, Yamaguchi. At Japan she had to take her husband's ashes to Ohtami Temple of Kyoto.

At the cruise journey, she met a Buddhist minister from Kona, Hawaii. Knowing her sufferings the Buddhist minister offered to carry her husband urn. She decided that she would visit him at the temple in few months.

Madam Hawayo's visit to health center and intimation of a drugless therapy, Reiki

Juggling with her ailments, after her sister's service she went for medical help at Akasak, Tokyo. There she was diagnosed with abdominal tumor. However, doctor found her too week for surgery. She was advised to restore some health to be operated.

After few weeks of rest she again visited the health center. The consultant surgeon fixed next day for the surgery.

Next day, in the morning, she was taken to the Operation Theater. There she was waiting to be operated. Amidst the serious mumbling of the doctors and nurses, she heard a voice in clarity, "This operation is not needed." Amazed she tried to find the source but she found none. She wished to listen it again. Then she heard it not once but thrice. Someone in clear voice had been advising her that the operation was not needed.

In her stillness, she felt as if she had been advised to clear her doubts with the surgeon.

She stepped down to the table in surgery robe. The nurses gathered around her in annoyance for messing up with operation preparation. They were cribbing at her.

The surgeon took her strange behavior as fright of operation. However, when she revealed the query to the surgeon, he got amazed. She asked him about other alternative therapy that did not need surgery.

The surgeon informed her about a drugless therapy. Nevertheless, he made it clear that he had no idea about how long the treatment could take to cure her.

She was advised by him to consult his sister. The surgeon's sister had been working at the hospital as a dietician.

She accompanied the surgeon's sister and visited to drugless therapy center. At the therapy center director's wife Mrs Hayashi and the receptionists received them.

It was a magnificently built building with beautiful garden. At the center of the building, there was a treatment hall. The hall was big enough to accommodate sixteen patients at a time. The patients had been getting treatment by the practitioners under the supervision of Dr Chujiro Hayashi.

Madam Hawayo treatment at the Reiki center

Hawayo got herself registered for treatment at the center. Two practitioners in the treatment hall attended her. The practitioners would heal her while placing their hands just above the body. During treatment sessions, they would often discuss about her ailments with such conviction as if they were witnessing them.

During one of the treatment sessions, one practitioner commented when he placed his hands above her stomach, "There is a lot of negativities at the point, there must be pain also." Then another commented, "Not only pain, there is tumor also." While scanning her body, they would comment about her breathing problem. Their comments about of ailments would amaze her. In her subsequent visit to the center, she decided to scrutinize everything around her. During the treatment, she would feel warmth on body parts. It would make her curious to find source of it. She had been expecting a connection of electric wire to practitioner hands as a source of heat.

In oriental set up of Japan, inquisitiveness on women's part was taken as bad etiquette. Therefore, Hawayo had to restrict her curiosity about Reiki treatment. However, due to Hawaiian brought up she could not restrict it for long.

Afterwards during one of her treatment sessions, she asked the practitioners about the hot sensations. They explained it as the vibrations of Reiki energy. To clear her disbelieve they rolled up their sleeves and showed their hands. There was not any wire connections in their hands.

Later she received few more facts about Reiki, but she was advised to restrict her curiosity till the completion of her treatment.

At the center, she noticed that patients would learn the method after their treatments. For many it was not possible to come every time to seek treatment for self and others during ailments. Hawayo too got interested in learning the technique after her treatment.

Madam Hawayo desired to learn Reiki

When she revealed her desire to learn the method after treatment she was discouraged by the practitioner. Since the Reiki teaching was only allowed for the citizen of Japan.

The denial of request disillusioned her. But Hawayo was not ready to give up so easily. Along with Reiki treatment Hawayo had also been taking meditation. During her meditation session she started praying for the guidance to learn Reiki.

She was not ready to leave Japan without divine Reiki learning that had cured her. After three weeks of Reiki treatment at the center, she asked for official permission to learn it. Since the Reiki teaching was only allowed to Japanese citizen. Therefore, her request was denied.

Nevertheless, she persisted citing the necessity of her cause. At last her entreaties were responded by the Reiki center. Hawayo was suggested to seek permission from Reiki association of Tokoyo.

To present her case adequately and highlighting the urgency of her need, she took help of the famed surgeon of the health center at Tokoyo. She got a recommendation letter from him. The surgeon strongly recommended her cause to Dr Hayashi. He intimated Dr Hayashi about acuteness of her ailments and her inability to come at the Reiki center repeatedly due to her financial constraints.

Dr Hayashi decided to honor the request of the renowned surgeon. Unanimously the Centre took her case as a special one and she was permitted to learn Reiki.

Reiki Initiation of Madam Hawayo

At the center, first she was made an honorary member of the center. Then under special condition, she got empowered with

Reiki initiation by Dr Hayashi.

She got four initiations in consecutive days. After initiation she had been taught to harness universal energy at her will. Then subsequently she learnt to heal and scan the body.

On her first treatment session, she was taught to treat the body above the neck. Subsequently she learnt to heal and scan head, eyes, ears, nose, throat, and the knots of negativities there.

On second day, she treated the front body -the chest, abdomen and all organs located there.

On third day, she dealt with back, which included spine, nervous system and organs. She was taught the right placement of hands on the body; shape the hands to receive energy for treatment.

On fourth day, Dr Hayashi discussed how to treat acute cases and explained the five percepts of Reiki and its importance.

For removal of effect, he stressed the need to remove of the cause.

The experience of Reiki treatment had given her idea about toxins removal from the body and its subsequent effect in restoration of health. As the treatment had ensued first her respiratory problems, then stones problem. After learning Reiki she decided to practice it for self-healing.

After six month, she went to Kyoto's temple for her husband's service. At that time, her parents were returning to Hawaii. After seeing them off to Hawaii she returned to Dr Hayashi's treatment center to work as a practitioner.

Madam Hawayo's life as Reiki Practitioner

At the center, she would start her day at early in the morning. With other sixteen practitioners, she would treat patients for five hours.

The afternoons were for the house calls that would sometime require her to take train journey for hours.

After accomplishment of outdoor duty she had to report it to Dr Hayashi. She continued that routine for a year. Barred from social life of family and friends, she got totally devoted to healing.

During the initial training year, she would accompany Dr Hayashi who would treat many influential persons. With passage of time her dedication to Reiki healing got recognized among the masses.

While treating her patients she would often recall the words of her sensei Dr Hayashi, "Remove the cause otherwise there shall be no effect." Then she would concentrate on the cause to mitigate the effect during the treatment.

When she had been staying at the center for the treatment, she never saw any person from lower strata getting treatment there. Therefore, a curiosity rose inside her to know the reason whether the poor was not allowed there.

She asked Dr Hayashi about it.

Dr Hayashi responded to her query laughingly. He explained her that to understand Reiki and its benefit, higher awareness was needed.

He explained. *"The people of higher consciousness have greater awareness. Even they can afford the best of treatment; instead they choose Reiki for its long lasting effect. Their awareness to the cause forces them to discard passivity easily. They take responsibility of self-cure and come forward to initiate action. Whereas a person of lower strata doubts its success and wants, a quick time bound cure for their invested money. Therefore people of lower strata don' seek Reiki for their cure."*

Madam Havayo returned to Hawaii

After her treatment and training for one year, Madam Takata returned to Hawaii in 1937. At Hawaii she was helped by Dr Hayashi to establish her clinic. He came to Hawaii with his daughters to help her.

She started her clinic at Honolulu in rented bungalows.

To create awareness about Reiki they arranged free lectures and demonstration. Japanese newspapers reported lectures and demonstrations of the drugless therapy Reiki. Articles on Reiki were published in Japanese news paper. Awareness about Reiki spread fast at the island.

Reiki awareness had been spreading fast. Therefore, in large number people started coming for Reiki treatment. After sometime, Mrs Takata had to arrange bigger hall to cater large gathering.

Dr Hayashi and his daughters stayed there for six months. In addition, in every possible way they helped her to create awareness about Reiki. He would give speeches and undertake demonstrations on Reiki healing.

In February 1938 at Hawaii, Dr Hayashi was felicitated by friends for allowing Reiki to reach the island. At the felicitation ceremony Dr Hayashi acknowledged Madame Takata's devotion to Reiki cause.

Through all trials and tribulations of life she not only was carrying Reiki healing but was actually living her life based on the Reiki percepts.

At that time to spread awareness about Reiki she had to undertake journey frequently. To aid her healing and enrich her knowledge of anatomy and physiology, she studied Varied Therapy at National College Drugless Physician. She completed studies in 1936.

Equipped with the knowledge, she started Reiki practice more actively.

Soon she got famed as Reiki practitioner. Due to her earnest work, she was invited at the biggest island of Hawaii to teach Reiki. She went to Kamnala (Warmea) to teach Reiki. In the beginning, people were not convinced about the success of Reiki treatment. Therefore, they wanted to test the authenticity of its healing power.

But she cured many acute patients at the island. The first patient was a lady with acute heart condition. Due to acuteness of her condition, she was unable to walk. Another was the patient of tonsillitis whose surgery was due in few weeks. Both of them intended to learn Reiki in case the treatment would work for them.

After Reiki treatment, both women were completely cured and they learnt it to practice it in their lives.

Spread of Reiki at the Hawaii islands

The news of their cure reached thick and fast on the island. Subsequently the willingness to learn Reiki by the people became overwhelming there. Witnessing the success of treatment, the hospital of plantation opened its door for Reiki. The response of communities was awe-inspiring. People from all corners of the islands came to enroll themselves for her teaching lessons.

She used to initiate people and treat them in large groups.

At the islands most of the people were engaged in farming. Therefore, to meet their needs Madame Takata would teach them to heal their seeds, crops, poultry or animals with Reiki energy for better returns. Touched with her devotion to cause, the people at the island would request her to visit them every six months. At her visit, more and more people would come to enroll themselves for Reiki lessons.

She would visit the island in a van and at the public places to teach Reiki.

In this way, she visited different places, healed every kind of ailments – from sore eyes to paralytic patients, and back injured person.

For acute patients she would advise family members to learn Reiki and help the patient to recover fast.

The effort of Reiki awareness by Madame Takata made it accessible to everyone at the Island of Hawaii.

She would teach people the different ways of Reiki treatment at Hilo. She would show them how Reiki works on animate things – on plants, birds, animals and human being.

Madam Hawayo premonition about her Sensei transition

In 1940, one night she saw Dr Hayashi in dream. Wearing a formal white kimono , he was walking at the Reiki center's hall at Tokoyo.

In next few weeks, she felt that she must visit Japan to meet him. However, after some pretext or others her visit postponed. Ultimately in April when she visited him in Tokyo. There she came to knew that the grand master was not well. Though Dr Hayashi was delighted after seeing her, yet he was surprised by her unexpected visit. He told her that he too wanted to see her.

He advised her to study hydrotherapy to aid her Reiki practice. During her stay in Japan visit, she came to know about Dr Hayashi decision to undertake transition.

After her hydrotherapy training, she returned to Dr Hayashi center. She knew that the grandmaster was not well.

At breakfast, Mrs Hayashi's welcomed her. Though everyone was aware of Dr Hayashi decision for his transition still as usual, everyone seemed cheerful and pleasant at the table.

Dr Hayashi told her that at 10 a.m. more people would visit him. He intended Madame Takata to take care of their visitors.

Then she realized it was time of her sensei's transition. She greeted everyone who were coming from all over places to witness his transition.

She was wondering on the calmness and composure of her sensei before his transition.

It was informed to her that the time of his transition fixed on 1.20p.m.

Before his transition, Dr Hayashi distributed and settled his responsibilities and properties. He had given the work of Reiki practice to Madame Takata as his daughters were then married and were settled in matrimony. They had shown their unwillingness to carry the work of Reiki. His son was already involved in business. He hadn't any leisure to devote for Reiki. His wife had intended to retire to country home.

As a result Madame Takata became an undisputed choice to carry the work of Reiki. Though it was an honorary position, the Tokyo property with clinic and house to carry out the Reiki work was given to Madame Takata with all requisite documents as his successor.

During his transition, in a composed way the family members were accepting the ultimate truth of life.

At around one o'clock Dr Hayashi entered in the hall. He was attired in a formal white silk kimono. His walk on the mattress was making a swishing sound as Madame Takata had seen him in her dream.

When he entered the hall he greeted everyone present over there. He explained them about his decision of transition.

At that time the war was inevitable between America and Japan. And as Naval Reserve Officer, it was likely for him to be called for active duty during the war. The job could have involved killing of people. Living the life of non- violence as Reiki practitioner he had long been renounced the violence. Living on the percepts of Reiki, it was impossible for him to involve in the war. Thus as a living example of Reiki life he decided to take transition from the world in perfect health, at the age of 62. After a long peaceful life he chose his transition.

He thanked everyone to make their presence for him. He explained the meaning of death as great change. He explained the immortality of soul.

All of them present in the hall witnessed the sign of his transition. The first sign came and went painlessly then twice it came. The third sign came as final and he fell in the open arm of Mrs Hayashi. During his transition his face was peaceful.

After his transition his body was taken to Reiki center of Tokyo and kept there for a week for public homage. People from different corners of Japan and Tokyo came to pay homage to the departed soul. During the week, no sign of deterioration was there in the body. According to Zen faith, after seven days he was cremated.

For Madame Takata it was a dual responsibility to raise her daughters and to manage the work of Reiki. Thus, she requested Mrs Hayashi to supervise the Reiki center of Tokyo. She obliged Madame Hawayo's request.

Life of Hawayo Takata as Reiki Practitioner and Reiki master

In this way an era of Reiki life started for Madame Takata. She shuttled in between Hawaii and Japan actively pursuing the job of Reiki.

After Second World War when she returned to Dr Hayashi Reiki Center in Tokyo, she found Mrs Hayashi at the center. Though everything around the Reiki Center had been turned to ruin, it was the only intact building amidst the ruins of bombing.

During the war, Mrs Hayashi turned the center into shelter home for the refugees and the quarters were given to families of homeless as shelter.

The orphaned teen girls had been taking in- house sewing training at the center. Feeling a bit hesitant, Mrs Hayashi apologized to Madame Takata for converting the Reiki center as refugees' shelter. She was apologetic to her for the interruption of Reiki work during the war. But Mrs Hayashi selfless approach to help humanity gained more confidence to Madame Takata. She appreciated her work of humanity and praised her approach towards life.

She returned the property of Tokyo to her and promised to spread Reiki to the world.

Thus undergoing the upheaval of war Dr Usui system of Reiki spread and took its roots in different part of the world.

Madame Takata returned to Honolulu from Hilo

After a decade Madam Takata returned to Honolulu from her Reiki Center at Hilo. At Honolulu she stayed for next twenty years and continued the work of Reiki.

Still she was travelling to different parts of island to take Reiki classes and on few occasions, she had visited mainland of America.

During 1963, she was invited to teach Reiki at Washington. Again her busy schedule started. For seven years, she travelled to different parts of the world to teach Reiki.

The Reiki awareness was spreading thick and fast. There was the need of more practitioner of Reiki. She started teaching her students to work as practitioners. In her lifetime, she initiated twenty-two Reiki Masters. She went to transition in Dec 1980.

Eight decades of Madame Takata's life and her personality

In her eight decades of life Madame Takata had contributed 45 years to Reiki. She spread the light of life on the planet.

Though she was an octogenarian but her skin and persona would defy her age. A fast-paced walk, alert mind and decisive actions were her alluring attributes. There were very few wrinkles on her face. Her grey hair would tell sign of her aging.

Living on the percepts of Reiki, with her upright life, she had acquired graceful mannerism and distinctive personality.

Devoted herself to the cause of Reiki even in the busiest of her schedule she would spread her hands for people to give Reiki. She would often say, "It is better to have some Reiki than none."

She had opted for simple way of life- she would wear simple dresses and would eat simple traditional food.

Nonetheless, her life was full of trials and tribulations but she worked on them and remedied it.

After Reiki initiation, people expect plain and easy life but life is never easy. It is always full of uncertainties. Reiki teaches us to deal with it strongly because stronger the person better s/he sails the uncertainties.

Reiki enables one to get required efficiency to handle the uncertainties.

The life of Madame Takata also shows her way of learning and exploring the life. Life is all about creating more opportunities of growth and opulence in life.

She not only healed and taught people but also counseled them to handle obstacles of lives. She would affirm her faiths in goodness and good deeds. She would say whatever you would give that would come to you.

She was a humble, soft-spoken woman of Oriental lineage. However, in her class her authoritative softness would rule the mind of learners. She would often teach the students to feel the energy and vibrations during Reiki treatment and scan negativities to clear the knots of ailment.

Her method of teaching was traditional. It was oral and based on practice. As a teacher, she knew how to command attention of the class.

She was an active woman with quiet and alert mind. Her assumptions about people and circumstances were hard to defy.

She was earnest about her work therefore she never allowed anyone to take it lightly. She taught Reiki as an authority and expected same commitment from the students.

Dr Hayashi - a follower of Dr Usui

When Dr Usui had large following of the students, Dr Hayashi was one of his most dedicated students.

After the transition of Dr Usui as a Reiki Grand Master, he carried the traditional teaching method of Dr Usui. After much thought, to spread Reiki to large masses he did set his clinic at Tokyo.

He was from an illustrious family and belonged to the place Atami in Japan.

His clinic got quick attention at Tokyo as it was the place of educated and influential people. They were ready to take charge of their well-being. Thus, person from affluent and educated families came forward for Reiki.

The journey of Reiki healing from Dr Usui to Dr Hayashi took long leap in a short span of time. The journey of Reiki Healing that started from beggars' slum reached mansions and palaces in a few years. The **mansions and palaces** show here realm of **higher awareness** and the **slums** show **lower realm** of mind. To receive Reiki higher awareness is needed, thus,

Just for the moment

Set aside all your condition

Make yourself empty for the moment.

Be open

And Receive it.

About The Author

The Author- Mrs. Arpana Kumar is a Reiki Master, Post Graduate Teacher of Life Sciences, and a passionate Writer.